MAGELLAN

EXPEDITION

A VOYAGE AROUND THE WORLD

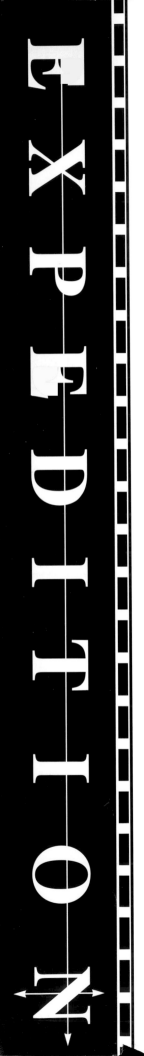

Editor April McCroskie
Technical Advisor Mark Whitchurch

First published in 1997 by Franklin Watts
96 Leonard Street London EC2A 4RH

First American edition 1998 by
Franklin Watts
A Division of Grolier Publishing
ShermanTurnpike
Danbury, CT 06816

10 9 8 7 6 5 4 3 2

ISBN 0-531-14454-2 (lib.bdg.) 0-531-15341-X (pbk.)

A copy of the Cataloging-in-Publication Data is
available from the Library of Congress

FIONA MACDONALD
studied history at Cambridge University and at the
University of East Anglia. She has also taught in
schools and adult education, contributed to television
programmes, and is the author of many books for
children on historical topics.

MARK BERGIN
was born in Hastings in 1961. He studied at
Eastbourne College of Art and has specialized in
historical reconstruction since leaving art school in
1983. He lives in Sussex with his wife and children.

DAVID SALARIYA
was born in Dundee, Scotland. He has designed and
created many new series of children's books. In 1989,
he established The Salariya Book Company Ltd.
He lives in Brighton with his wife, the illustrator
Shirley Willis, and their son Jonathan.

MAGELLAN
A Voyage Around the World

Written by FIONA MACDONALD

Illustrated by MARK BERGIN

Created and designed by
DAVID SALARIYA

W

FRANKLIN WATTS
A Division of Grolier Publishing
NEW YORK • LONDON • HONG KONG • SYDNEY
DANBURY, CONNECTICUT

CONTENTS

INTRODUCTION

ERDINAND MAGELLAN lived from 1480-1522. He spent most of his career as an army officer, living and fighting abroad, but he went on to become one of the greatest sailors of the 16th century. Magellan lived at a time when, throughout Europe, there was enormous interest in exploring far-away lands.

In 1511, Magellan made the voyage around Africa and across the Indian Ocean to the far-away Spice Islands (part of present-day Indonesia). He was the first European explorer to sail westwards around America and reach the Pacific Ocean. He proved, beyond doubt, that the world was round, not flat.

He also discovered, to his dismay, that the route pioneered by earlier sailors, eastwards around Africa to the rich Spice Islands, was shorter, quicker, and safer than the westward route he had set out to explore.

Magellan did not live to complete his planned voyage around the world. He died far away from home, in a Pacific island war. But his voyage was continued by another experienced sea captain who brought Magellan's ship the *Vittoria* safely round the world and back to Spain. This epic voyage was the first-ever circumnavigation of the world.

The Silk Road

Goods were carried long distances overland on horseback and by camel caravans. Traders traveled along the old Silk Road – a network of tracks that linked Europe and Asia. There were trading posts along the way, too.

Trade Secrets

Silk and fine porcelain were among the most highly-prized goods carried from China along the Silk Road. For many centuries, both silk and porcelain were made by secret processes, unknown to Europeans.

S INCE 1418 Portuguese sailors had been exploring the west coast of Africa looking for gold, slaves and a trade route to the east. They hoped to find a route around southern Africa. Many people thought ships sailing so far south would be burnt up by the sun or swept away by big waves. But in 1487-1488 Portuguese explorer Bartolomeu Dias sailed into the Indian Ocean. Then, in 1492, Christopher Columbus, an Italian with Spanish backing, set off across the Atlantic hoping to reach the rich lands of the east by traveling west.

Map of the known world in 1490, by German scholar Henricus Martellus.

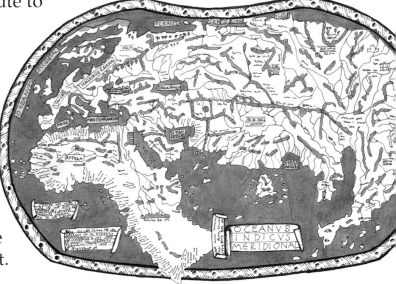

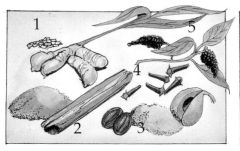

Exotic Spices

Spices from Asia sold for high prices in Europe:
1 Ginger.
2 Cinnamon. 3 Nutmeg.
4 Cloves. 5 Black Pepper.

The Spice Route

Asian spices were carried from the Spice Islands by Arabian traders who sailed across the Indian Ocean in graceful ships, called dhows.

Medicines

Plants like opium poppies (for pain relief) and rhubarb (a laxative) were imported to Europe from Asian lands to be used in medicines.

A Famous Voyage
In 1492, Christopher Columbus set sail with three ships, hoping to reach the rich lands of Asia by sailing west. Instead, he arrived in the Americas, which soon became known to Europeans as the "New World".

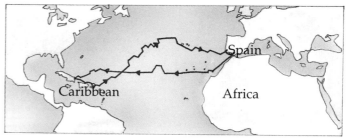

Christopher Columbus
In 1492, Columbus sailed from southern Spain to the islands of the Bahamas in the Caribbean. His voyage took 61 days. Between 1493-1504, Columbus made three more voyages across the Atlantic Ocean.

Christopher Columbus claimed the "new" lands he explored for the King and Queen of Spain.
Today, we know that Columbus had reached America, but when he died in 1506, he believed he had reached Japan.

African Trading Posts
In the 15th century, Portuguese sailors and explorers began to build forts and trading settlements along the West African coast.

Sailor Prince
Henry the Navigator of Portugal (1394-1460) funded many voyages by Portuguese explorers. He had a library of maps and travel books.

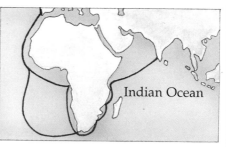

Sailing to India
In 1487-1488, Bartolomeu Dias sailed round the Cape of Good Hope and into the Indian Ocean. Vasco da Gama reached India in 1498.

•SHIPBUILDING AND REPAIRS•

Shipbuilding
1. Choosing the Timber
Tough, slow-growing oak was the best timber to use for shipbuilding. Expert shipbuilders visited the forest to choose the most suitable trees. Trees were felled with an iron-bladed ax.

2. Transporting the Timber
All the leaves, twigs, and side branches were lopped off the felled oak tree trunks. They were then ready to be transported to the shipyard in heavy wagons pulled by teams of cart-horses.

TO SAILORS strolling on the docks in Seville, Spain, the ship *Vittoria* (*Victory*) did not seem worth a second glance. Like other 16th-century ships, it was made of wood, with tough canvas sails. The *Vittoria* was old and sea-worn. Its timbers bore the scars of wild storms and many repairs. Yet ships like this were all Magellan could afford. He had bought five to take with him on his adventurous voyage.

In spite of the *Vittoria*'s shabbiness and age, it was destined to win a place in history. It became the first ship to sail right around the world.

The Vittoria

Caravels
Caravels were small, sleek ships with lateen (triangular) sails. They were designed to be easy to maneuver in tricky coastal waters.

Hulls
The hulls of caravels (*above*, *left*) and carracks (*above*) were built in carvel style. Planks of wood were laid down and fitted together.

Carracks
Carracks were huge ships with big, square sails. They were designed to carry valuable cargo in their wide hulls. They went on long ocean voyages.

•A GUIDE TO BUILDING TECHNIQUES•

3. At the Sawpits

The bark was removed from the trunks, and then they were cut into square sections at the sawpits, using a two-handed saw. One man stood above the tree trunk, the other stood in the pit below. Sawing was exhausting work.

4. At the Workshop

Carpenters trimmed the sawn planks of wood into the shapes needed to build the ship. They used knives or a sharp tool called an adze. Planks for the ship's hull were curved into shape by steaming them over boiling water.

Ships were built around a "backbone" of strong timber, called a keel. Then curved pieces of wood, called "ribs", were joined to it, making a framework for the curved timbers of the hull.

Keel ✍

Ribs

Hull

Rope-Making

Strands of tough fibers from hemp plants were twisted together to make rope. This was done in long courtyards called ropewalks.

Caulking

Hemp fibers were packed tightly into any gaps in the ship's hull. The fibers were coated with tar to keep water out. This was called caulking.

Shipbuilder's Tools

1 Drawknife for shaping planks. 2 Adze. 3 Ax.
4 Saw. 5 Auger (hole-borer).
6 Chisels. 7 Mallet. 8 Plane.
9 Caulking iron.

•MAPS AND COMPASSES•

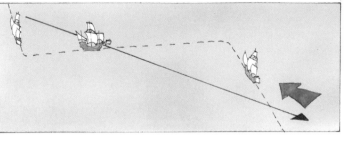

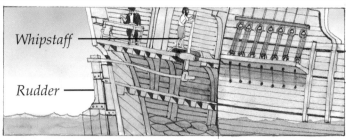

Whipstaff

Rudder

Against the Wind

It was difficult for sailing ships, which relied on the wind in their sails to push them along, to travel in the opposite direction to the way the wind was blowing. They had to steer a zigzag course. This was called tacking.

Keeping on Course

Ships were steered by using a rudder – a huge underwater paddle at the stern (back of the ship). The rudder was connected to a long wooden lever, called a whipstaff, operated by a sailor standing on deck.

FOR MAGELLAN and his sailors, steering a ship was a matter of life and death. If they strayed from their planned course, they might run aground on sandbanks or be smashed to pieces on dangerous coastal rocks. They had only simple navigation equipment to help them and, in the early 16th century, very unreliable maps.

Once ships were out of sight of land, it was vital for sailors to know their exact position. If they got lost at sea they might never find dry land again. They would die as soon as their ship's supply of food and water ran out.

Plotting a course

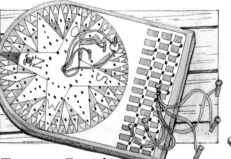

Traverse Board

A traverse board was marked with a compass-like pattern, and had holes. A peg was put into a hole every 30 minutes to record a ship's course.

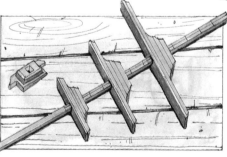

Cross-Staff

A cross-staff was used to work out latitude – the position north or south of the equator. It measured the angle of the sun above the horizon.

Astrolabe

An astrolabe was a metal disc fitted with "pointers" that moved to measure the height of the sun above the horizon and so work out latitude.

Log line

Lead line

Speed and Depth

Speed was measured by a log line – a reel of knotted rope trailing behind the ship. The faster the reel unwound, the faster the ship was traveling. Depth was measured with a lead line – a weighted rope thrown overboard.

The "Three Ls"

Sailors relied on the "Three Ls" – log line, lead line and landmarks – to steer a course. Lead lines and landmarks were only useful in shallow waters, or in sight of the coast. Other instruments were needed in deep waters.

Senior members of the ship's crew worked together to calculate the ship's course and steer along it accurately. They also kept a written record of where they had sailed in a diary, called a "log".

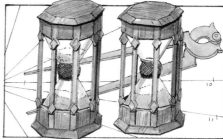

Armillary Sphere

This was a model of the sky, showing stars and planets. It helped sailors out of sight of land to work out their position by looking at stars overhead.

Magnetic Compass

This contained a needle of magnetized metal that always pointed North. It helped sailors work out where to steer their ship.

Hour Glass

This was used to measure time. The upper glass chamber was filled with sand. It took 30 minutes for the sand to trickle into the chamber below.

Noble Soldier
Ferdinand Magellan was born in 1480 in Porto, northern Portugal. He came from a minor noble family.

In the East
As a boy Magellan served as a page at the royal court. He then went on to become a soldier. In 1511-12, he served with the Portuguese army in Africa and the Far East. He fought against Moslem merchants in India and against the rulers of Malaya (part of modern Malaysia).

CHRISTOPHER COLUMBUS died believing he had reached Japan. But many people, including Magellan, knew this was wrong. Columbus had reached America. By 1517, Magellan had a bold new plan to sail around South America and find a sea route to India and China.

Magellan was Portuguese but he asked Portugal's enemy, King Charles of Spain, to sponsor his voyage. It was rumored that Magellan had quarreled with the Portuguese royal family, but we do not know for sure. King Charles gave Magellan money to equip five ships based at the Spanish port of Seville. By 1519, they were ready to sail.

Magellan with King Charles.

Portuguese India
The city of Calicut was built on the west coast of India by Portuguese explorers. By the end of the 16th century, it was one of the main centers of the international spice trade. It had a good harbor, well-guarded warehouses and comfortable homes for wealthy merchants and shipowners.

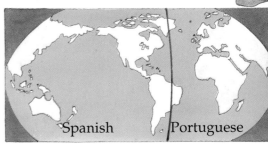

Spanish   Portuguese

Treaty of Tordesillas, 1494
This treaty was signed by Spain and Portugal. They agreed to split between themselves the land their explorers had claimed in America and the Far East.

The Marriage of Magellan

In 1517, Magellan married Beatrice, the daughter of a wealthy Portuguese merchant who traded in Spain. Beatrice's father helped Magellan get an introduction to the Spanish court.

Magellan's Royal Enemy

King Manuel of Portugal sent spies to join Magellan's crew. He wanted to sabotage Magellan's voyage because it was backed by Portugal's ancient enemy, King Charles of Spain.

King Manuel of Portugal tried to make sure that food supplies for the voyage were stale and mouldy.

Provisions for the Voyage

The ships were loaded with flour and salt to make bread, and about 550 pounds (250 kilograms) of hard, dry, ship's biscuit – the basic rations.

Water Supplies

The ships were stocked with oak barrels full of fresh water, and 500 butts (large kegs) of wine. Rainwater provided valuable extra water supplies.

Plenty of Meat

Magellan bought dried fish and meat preserved in salt water. Around 6,060 pounds (2750 kilograms) of salt pork were taken on the voyage.

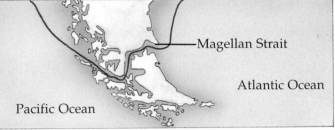

Magellan Strait

Atlantic Ocean

Pacific Ocean

A Way Round?

Magellan was taking a great risk in trying to sail westwards round the world. As this 16th-century map shows, many people thought that a vast, unknown southern continent would block his way.

The Magellan Strait

Magellan's journey was not halted by the mysterious "southern continent". In fact, he found a narrow sea passageway, leading from the Atlantic to the Pacific. Today, this seaway is called the Magellan Strait.

FEW 16TH-CENTURY SAILORS were willing to take part in a voyage into the unknown. So Magellan had to recruit his crew from desperate, disreputable men whom no one else would employ. He did not tell them his plans, so when they realized they were going around the world, they tried to mutiny and turn back. Magellan hanged the ringleaders and sailed on.

Magellan did persuade a few well-trained sea captains, like Juan Sebastian del Cano, to sail with him. Some young Spanish nobles also joined the voyage. They all hoped to make their fortunes in the Spice Islands.

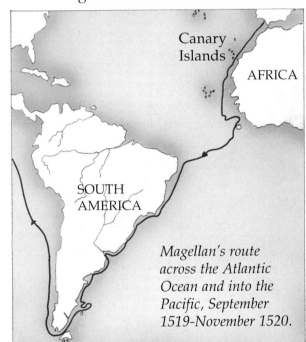

Canary Islands

AFRICA

SOUTH AMERICA

Magellan's route across the Atlantic Ocean and into the Pacific, September 1519-November 1520.

Bad News

Magellan called at Tenerife, in the Canary Islands. His father-in-law told him that Portuguese spies on his ships were planning to kill him.

In the Doldrums

The ships got stuck in the doldrums – part of the south Atlantic Ocean where it is often calm. Without wind, the sailing ships could not move.

Holiday Ashore

Magellan's ships finally arrived off the coast of Brazil. The crew was tired and angry, so Magellan gave them a holiday on shore.

• CALMS, STORMS, AND MUTINY •

Sea Creatures

Magellan and his crew saw all kinds of sea creatures in the southern oceans: 1 Manta Rays. 2 Flying fish. 3 Penguins. 4 Whales. 5 Seals. 6 Porpoises. 7 Squid. They trailed lines over the side of the ship to catch the fish.

Monsters of the Deep

All the sea creatures they saw proved to be harmless, but many of Magellan's sailors were still frightened of meeting the savage "monsters of the deep" they had heard about in earlier travelers' tales.

Off the coast of Argentina, Magellan's ships were caught in a violent storm. One of them, The Santiago, *was wrecked. Soon afterwards, the crew of another ship, the* San Antonio, *deserted him and headed back to Spain. They took most of the fleet's food supplies with them.*

Mutiny

The weather was cold and wet as they sailed south. The crew mutinied – they wanted to go home. Magellan hanged all the trouble makers.

Through the Strait

Magellan sighted the entrance to a strait (narrow seaway) leading to the Pacific. It took them 38 days to sail along it – the first Europeans to do so.

Magellan in the Pacific

At first the water was calm, so he called it the Pacific Ocean ("pacific" means "peaceful"). But soon he was in some of the world's stormiest waters.

15

•THE PACIFIC•

Unknown Waters
Magellan's fleet was now reduced to only three ships. They set sail in good weather across the Pacific Ocean. But these were unknown waters and none of the crew knew what lay ahead.

M AGELLAN'S ships left South America and sailed northwest across the Pacific for 3 months and 20 days. Food supplies ran out, and the little water they had left on board was stale and polluted. Many of the sailors died.

After a nightmare voyage, they finally reached the remote island of Guam, in the western Pacific. Magellan and his crew were very lucky to find land and food in time. Their ships might have sailed for months across the vast Pacific Ocean without sighting land.

The Open Seas
At first, the crew was hopeful, but days and then weeks passed without any sight of land. Were they sailing to their doom? They had no maps or charts to help them steer as no Europeans had sailed here before.

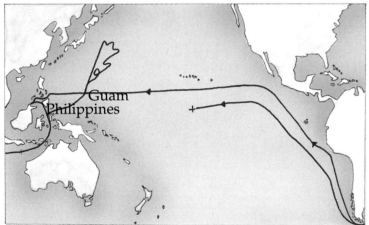

Magellan's voyage, from the tip of South America to the Philippines, November 1520-March 1521. In January 1521 they sighted land, but could not find any shallow water in which to anchor.

Disappointment Island
In January 1521, the crew sighted land, but there was no harbor, and they could not drop anchor. They named it "Disappointment Island".

Island of Thieves
On 6 March 1521, Magellan's ships reached safe anchorage off the island of Guam. Local people kept stealing from the ships so the crew sailed on.

Safe at Last
Magellan's crew was still weak and ill. Thankfully, after a short voyage, on 16 March, they found another safe anchorage in sheltered waters.

Mice For Sale
Everyone on board feared they would die of hunger and thirst before they reached land. They ate anything they could find, including sawdust, leather, and insects. Mice were sold for half a ducat (a solid gold coin) each.

Scurvy
Many sailors fell ill with scurvy – a deadly disease caused by lack of vitamin C. Magellan stayed fit and well, probably because of his private supply of quince marmalade, made from vitamin-rich fruit.

Scurvy was a miserable disease. Sailors' gums bled, their teeth fell out, their joints swelled and ached, and their bodies became covered in sores. On the voyage across the Pacific, 20 members of Magellan's crew died of scurvy. Today we know that eating lots of fruit prevents scurvy.

On the Island of Cebu
Friendly local people gave Magellan and his crew palm oil, bananas, coconuts, and fish. The sailors ate and rested to build up their strength.

Exchanging Gifts
In return for their kindness, food, and shelter, Magellan gave the Cebu islanders gifts of bells, mirrors, and lengths of brightly colored cloth.

A New Name
Magellan renamed Cebu and the neighboring islands "the Philippines", in honor of Crown Prince Philip, son of the King of Spain.

•MURDER•

Making Converts
Magellan and the King of Cebu gave each other gifts and became friends. Magellan converted the king to Christianity and, in a splendid ceremony, 800 islanders were baptized as Christians, too.

A Local War
Magellan spent many hours with the King of Cebu. He learned that the king had quarreled with a nearby ruler, and that Cebu soldiers were getting ready to fight. Magellan died fighting in this local war.

MAGELLAN and his crew were treated very kindly in the Philippines. By offering them food and shelter, the islanders saved their lives. So in return, Magellan promised to help the King of Cebu fight against enemies on the neighboring island of Mactan. Magellan felt sure his soldiers' guns and swords would defeat the local people's spears.

But, tragically, Magellan was wrong. Along with 40 of his men, he was stabbed to death in the battle against the Mactan islanders. He was mourned by his men as a "brave and noble captain".

Magellan baptizes the Cebu islanders as Christians.

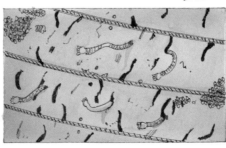

Rotting Timbers
Shortly after Magellan's death, the crew discovered that the ship *Concepcion* was rotten. As soon as they loaded it with cargo, it began to sink.

Dangerous Worms
The *Concepcion's* hull had been eaten away by teredo worms. The worms bored holes in the wooden planks, causing them to crack and crumble.

Burnt On Shore
After inspecting the *Concepcion's* rotten timbers, the crew decided to burn the whole ship. It was not possible to repair it.

•THE DEATH OF MAGELLAN•

A New Commander
After Magellan's death, the whole crew was in a state of shock. A Portuguese nobleman from among his crew, named Juan Lopes Carvalho, took command. He was an experienced ships' pilot.

Jealousy
Carvalho was jealous of Magellan's success. He wanted to claim all the credit for the voyage for himself. It was reported that he destroyed Magellan's log book, so no one would know what Magellan had achieved.

Magellan and some of his crew were trapped ashore by Mactan warriors. Bravely, Magellan told his men to leave him, and to save their own lives.

Tropical Diseases
Although they were now well-fed, many of the crew fell victim to tropical diseases like malaria. They died and were buried on the beach.

Two Ships Remain
There were now only two of Magellan's five ships left – the *Trinidad* and the *Vittoria*. Only about 108 of Magellan's original crew survived.

Pirates
Led by Carvalho, the crew spent two months as pirates. They robbed villagers and captured local sailors to help them sail their ships.

Setting Sail Again

After quarreling with the local people, Carvalho and the crew decided to leave the Philippines. In June 1521, they set sail for the Spice Islands in the *Trinidad* and the *Vittoria*. They robbed local people along the way.

Arriving in Port

By November, the *Trinidad* and the *Vittoria* had reached the Spice Islands. They were laden with loot after their spell of piracy. Local sailors and traders hurried to meet them in outrigger canoes.

MAGELLAN WAS DEAD, but his voyage around South America and across the Pacific had established that it was possible to reach the Far East by sailing west.

Now, in summer 1521, the surviving members of the crew decided to sail south from the Philippines to the rich Spice Islands. They wanted to load their ships with cloves, nutmeg, and mace, before sailing home. After the fight on Mactan, they no longer felt friendly towards the local people. So they kidnapped some of them and forced them to sail with them and show them the way.

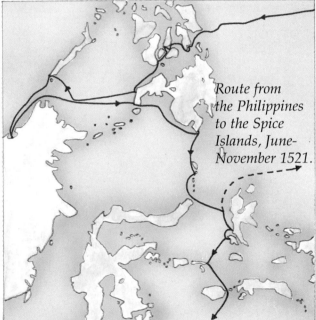

Route from the Philippines to the Spice Islands, June-November 1521.

Buying Spices

The Spice Islands produced the world's best nutmeg, cloves and mace. The crew bought these valuable spices to sell when they got home.

Silks and Pearls

As well as spices, Magellan's crew also purchased precious silks, lustrous pearls, and beautiful tropical birds from merchants in the Spice Islands.

Perfumes and Drugs

The Spice Islands produced drugs like bitter aloes, used in medicines for stomach problems, and sandalwood, for making perfumes.

• A FORTUNE TO BE MADE •

Royal Welcome

The Sultan of Ternate sent out his magnificent royal barge to inspect the newly-arrived ships. He was suspicious of these ragged, greedy sailors but allowed them to trade. But their good fortune did not last long.

The crowded harbor of Ternate was one of the busiest trading ports in the Spice Islands.

Del Cano Takes Charge

In the Spice Islands, Carvalho and many other members of the crew died of fever. Juan Sebastian del Cano, an experienced sailor from the Basque country in northern Spain, took command of the *Vittoria*.

Back to Europe

In December 1521, del Cano decided to return to Europe. He got ready to sail in the *Vittoria*. The *Trinidad* stayed behind for urgent repairs.

Heading Home

When the *Trinidad* was finally repaired it set out across the Pacific Ocean. The voyages back for both ships were long, difficult and very dangerous.

Fear of Capture

Magellan's crew feared meeting the Portuguese in the Spice Islands. They knew Portuguese soldiers would capture or kill them.

•SAILING HOME•

Sole Survivor

The *Vittoria* began its long journey home in December 1521, sailing westward around the tip of Africa. It was 28 months since it had set sail from Spain and though the return journey was shorter it was just as hazardous.

Captain del Cano

Del Cano was the senior surviving captain, so he planned the *Vittoria*'s homeward voyage. On board with him were 47 sailors from Magellan's original crew, plus 13 Indonesian sailors recruited from the Spice Islands.

JUAN SEBASTIAN DEL CANO decided that the *Trinidad* and the *Vittoria* must leave the Spice Islands before they became too fragile to sail. In December 1521, del Cano sailed west across the Indian Ocean in the *Vittoria*. After the *Trinidad* was mended, it was loaded with 55 tons of cloves and set off across the Pacific. But it met contrary winds, and many of the crew died of scurvy. The *Trinidad* returned to the Spice Islands, but it was captured by the Portuguese and the crew was imprisoned. Only four of them got back to Spain.

The Vittoria's *route home from the Spice Islands to Europe, December 1521-September 1522. It sailed across the Indian Ocean and around southern Africa, then on to the Cape Verde Islands in the Atlantic Ocean.*

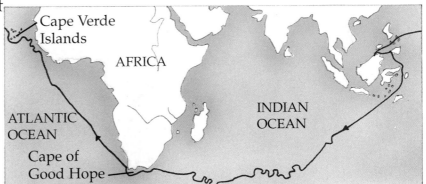

Cape Verde Islands

AFRICA

ATLANTIC OCEAN

Cape of Good Hope

INDIAN OCEAN

Cape of Good Hope

At the Cape, del Cano steered too far south. The *Vittoria* was buffeted by fierce gales and mountainous waves, and was almost wrecked by icebergs.

Flying Fish

In the wild South Atlantic Ocean, the crew often saw spectacular sights such as huge whales, and flying fish that followed the ship.

Ill and Tired

In May 1522, they reached the Cape of Good Hope again. But now their stocks of food were running dangerously low, and the crew were ill and tired.

To Africa

It took the *Vittoria* over two months to cross the Indian Ocean. In February 1522, the sailors caught sight of the East African coast. But they did not dare to land, in case they met Portuguese soldiers there.

Desperate for food, the Vittoria *anchored briefly in a sheltered bay on the West African coast early in May 1522. But the sailors were scared of being attacked by local people.*

Mistakes

Del Cano was not as good a navigator as Magellan had been and often made mistakes. One mistake at the Cape of Good Hope (at the tip of South Africa) added days to the voyage.

Across the Equator

The *Vittoria* crossed the Equator on 8 June. But most of the crew were ill and 15 men had died already. By 9 July the crew had run out of food.

At Cape Verde

The ship landed at the Cape Verde Islands, even though these islands belonged to the Portuguese. The sailors traded spices for fruit and rice.

Captured

The Portuguese sent soldiers to arrest the crew of the *Vittoria*. Thirteen of them were captured and marched off to prison.

•HOME AT LAST•

Almost Home

In August 1522, the *Vittoria* sailed past the Azores – a group of Portuguese islands in the Atlantic Ocean. But the sea-worn *Vittoria* was beginning to leak. Would it survive to complete the journey?

Reaching Seville

On 8 September 1522, the *Vittoria* turned inland from the sea, and sailed up the Guadalquivir River towards the port of Seville in Spain. The sailors cheered – they were nearly home!

O N 8 SEPTEMBER 1522, longshoremen and sailors at work on the docks in the port of Seville started as if they had seen a ghost. What battered, leaking ship was this, sailing up the river? And who were the ragged, half-starved crew – just 17 Europeans and 4 Spice Islanders? The *Vittoria* and its sailors had been away for so long, it seemed as if they were returning from the dead.

Once the people of Seville had got over their shock and surprise, del Cano and the survivors were given a heroes' welcome. But there was sadness, too, as many sailors had not returned home.

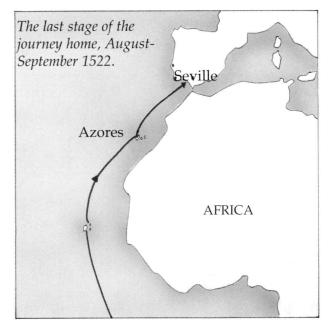

The last stage of the journey home, August–September 1522.

Seville

Azores

AFRICA

Astonishment

The citizens of Seville were astonished to see the *Vittoria* sail into harbor. Most people believed that the ship had sunk many months ago.

Welcome Home

For 17 members of Magellan's original crew, there were joyful reunions with families and friends. They had been away for almost three years.

Few Survivors

Most of Magellan's original crew had not survived. Out of the 270 men who had sailed with him, almost all had died during the voyage.

Giving Thanks

On September 9th, the day after the sailors arrived home in Seville, they walked in a solemn, barefoot procession through the city streets to the church of Santa Maria de la Vittoria.

Candles and Prayers

They lit candles in front of the church altar, and said prayers to thank God for their safe journey home. They knew they were very lucky to be alive.

The Vittoria *sails into Seville harbor at last.*

Set Free

The 13 sailors captured on the Cape Verde Islands also survived. They were freed and sent home a few days after the *Vittoria* reached Seville.

Congratulations

King Charles of Spain invited del Cano and all the crew to his royal palace. He wanted to congratulate them and learn about their travels.

Cloves for Sale

When the *Vittoria*'s cargo of cloves was sold, it only raised enough money to cover the costs of fitting out the five ships for Magellan's voyage.

•DEL CANO•

Enemies
Del Cano liked being a hero. He bought a new house and lots of new clothes. But his extravagant, boastful, selfish lifestyle made him many enemies. He had to employ a bodyguard to keep watch outside his door.

Coat of Arms
King Charles granted del Cano a coat of arms showing a globe decorated with cloves and cinnamon sticks.

A Forgotten Hero
Few people praised Magellan's courage during the voyage, or even remembered his heroic death.

Back home del Cano fell in love with two women, and entertained friends with stories of his adventures.

THE *VITTORIA*'S record-breaking voyage would not have happened without Magellan's original idea, and his courage and determination to make it happen.

Yet on his return to Spain, del Cano took all the credit for sailing the *Vittoria* around the world, and blamed Magellan for everything that had gone wrong with the voyage. But in 1529, King Charles proclaimed that Magellan was not to blame.

Today, we remember Magellan, del Cano, and the sailors on the *Vittoria* for a great achievement – the first voyage around the world.

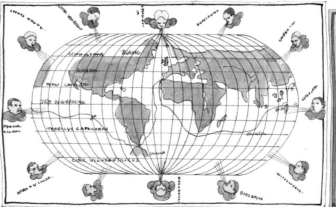

World Globes
Magellan and del Cano proved beyond all doubt that the earth was round. Soon, geographers and craftworkers began to make globes like this.

New Maps
This 16th-century map of the world (*above*), drawn by Italian cartographer Battista Agnese, shows the *Vittoria*'s route around the world.

Antonio Pigafetta
A sailor on the voyage wrote a book about his adventures. Its front cover (*above*) showed Pacific islands and a ship fitted like a Pacific outrigger canoe.

Trade Winds

Trade winds blow in a regular pattern across the Pacific Ocean, in one direction only, from America to Asia.

These winds helped Magellan's ships reach the Philippines from South America, by blowing them on their way. But the same winds made it difficult and dangerous to cross the Pacific Ocean in the opposite direction.

Sailors had to battle against the winds for most of the voyage. This added to the length of the voyage, and few ships had room to carry enough supplies.

The next successful voyage around the world did not take place for more than 50 years. In 1577, English pirate and explorer Francis Drake set sail from Plymouth. Like Magellan and del Cano, Drake sailed westwards across the Atlantic, across the Pacific, and around southern Africa. His ship, the Golden Hind, *finally returned home in 1580.*

Hopes for Trade

The *Vittoria's* voyage inspired other explorers to plan new voyages. They hoped to make their fortunes by trading with the rich Spice Islands.

Del Cano's Second Voyage

In 1525, del Cano hoped to circumnavigate the world again. This was brave, after the hardships and dangers of his first trip round the world.

Del Cano Dies

Like many of the sailors on his earlier voyage, del Cano died of disease during the journey across the Pacific Ocean. He was buried at sea in 1525.

*I*N THE SHORT TERM Magellan's voyage round the world had been a disaster, and it had failed to make a profit. But Magellan's murder, the deaths among the crew, and the three years of the *Vittoria*'s voyage all showed that the westward journey to the Spice Islands was much longer and much more dangerous than the better-known eastwards voyage around the tip of Africa and across the Indian Ocean.

*T*HE DISCOVERY of the trade winds also discouraged most other sailors from copying Magellan's voyage. They realized that if they headed westwards from Europe to the Spice Islands they could not turn back but would have to sail right around the world. After Magellan's and del Cano's experiences on board the *Vittoria*, that was not an inviting prospect! The Pacific Ocean's reputation as a place of death and danger was increased after 1525 when del Cano died there, trying to make a second exploration of the Pacific.

•WHAT HAPPENED NEXT?•

IT WAS NOT until 1565 that a Spanish sailor, Urdaneta, discovered a way of crossing the Pacific from Asia to America that avoided the trade winds. He sailed far north from the Spice Islands then headed for the west coast of America, skirting round the vast expanse of ocean where the trade winds blew. But it was still a long, dangerous voyage. Throughout the 16th century, adventurers, explorers and map makers concentrated on investigating North and South America. It was not until 1577 that Englishman Francis Drake dared to set off on another round-the-world voyage.

THERE WERE political disappointments, too, as a result of the *Vittoria*'s voyage. For years the rulers of Spain and Portugal had been quarreling over who had the right to claim the lands visited by Spanish and Portuguese explorers. They made an agreement in 1494, in the Treaty of Tordesillas, but, secretly, both sides hoped to claim extra lands.

BOTH Spain and Portugal wanted to prove that the Spice Islands belonged to them. But inaccurate 16th-century methods of measuring latitude at sea made it impossible to solve the dispute. Sailors were not able to measure latitude accurately for more than 200 years, until English clockmaker John Harrington invented a chronometer – a very accurate time-keeper – in 1759.

THE QUARREL over the Spice Islands ended finally in 1527, when King Charles V of Spain agreed to give up Spain's claims over them in return for a payment from Portugal of 350,000 solid gold coins. Charles made this agreement because he was running short of money to pay for fighting a war with France.

IN THE LONG TERM, Magellan and del Cano's round-the-world voyage was a success. It showed both men's courage and daring. It also proved, once and for all, that the world was round.

Caravans
Herds of specially trained camels, used to carry heavy loads for long distances over dry or desert land.

Caravels
Small, sleek ships, usually fitted with lateen (triangular) sails. They were designed to be fast and easy to steer in shallow coastal waters.

Carracks
Huge, slow-moving ships with big square sails. They were designed to carry large loads of valuable cargo in their wide, deep hulls. Merchants from Spain and Portugal sailed in carracks to trade with the Spice Islands and, later, the New World.

Cartographer
A map maker.

Circumnavigation
A round-the-world voyage.

Coat of arms
A special badge worn by noble people to display their family membership and high rank. Coats of arms were granted by rulers, as a reward for brave or pioneering actions. Usually they were decorated with pictures or patterns showing a noble family's achievements.

Exotic
Coming from far away lands.

Hemp
A tall plant with a tough, thick stem. Fibers from hemp stems were twisted together to make rope. They were also woven into hardwearing cloth, called canvas, which was used to make ships' sails.

Latitude
Position north or south of the equator – an imaginary line drawn around the widest part of the Earth.

Mace
A valuable spice grown only in tropical lands. Mace is the name given to the outer coating of nutmeg (*see below*). It has a slightly sweet, peppery flavor.

Mutiny
A rebellion by soldiers or sailors against the officers who command them.

Nutmeg
A valuable spice produced by trees growing in hot, moist climates. It has a warm, spicy flavor.

Porcelain
Very fine, white pottery made from a special kind of clay. In Magellan's time, it was only produced in China.

Scurvy
A serious disease caused by lack of vitamin C. It killed many sailors in Magellan's time. It can be prevented by eating fresh fruit and vegetables.

Spice Islands
A group of islands in present-day Indonesia. Because of their year-round hot weather and plentiful rainfall, the world's best quality spices were produced there.

Strait
A narrow channel where the sea runs between two land masses.

Tacking
Steering a zigzag course at sea. Tacking is the only way in which a sailing ship can travel in the opposite direction to the wind.

Trade winds
Winds that blow in one direction only for most of the year. The name "trade" comes from the word "trodden". People in the past said that the winds "trod" the same path.

INDEX